# DISCIP
# FROM INFORMATION TO

## Introduction

This workbook was written for the purpose of helping you maximize the concepts in the book, *Discipleship: From Information to Execution*. It is my desire to help you do more than simply gain information from the book, but rather to learn how to take that information and turn it into action in a way that will transform your life.

PERSONALIZE AND EXECUTE:

With each chapter, there is space for you to write out any of your own thoughts and reflections. This is to challenge you to engage with what you are reading and take time to respond through prayer and writing. After each chapter, there are also questions to help you personalize and execute the concepts in that chapter. The questions are to challenge you to personally reflect on what is being presented, as well as execute actions in your life.

DISCIPLING YOUR OWN SOUL:

You will learn as you read the book that an important part of discipleship is knowing how to use the Word to sanctify the soul. James 1:21 says, "Therefore lay aside all filthiness and overflow of wickedness, and receive with meekness the implanted word, which is able to save your souls." It is by the washing of the Word that we are able to drag our thoughts, emotions and will into alignment with His thoughts, emotions and will. James 1:22 goes further in the concept and implores us not just to know the Word, but to do the Word. "But be doers of the word, and not hearers only, deceiving yourselves." This is the whole shift that is discussed throughout the book and the reason for the name, *Discipleship: From Information to Execution*.

## "From The Author"

*"Every part of Scripture is God-breathed and useful one way or another – showing us truth, exposing our rebellion, correcting our mistakes, training us to live God's way.* **Through the Word we are put together and shaped up** *for the tasks God has for us." 2 Timothy 3:16-17, The Message (Emphasis mine)*

I think that we too often forget that the Scriptures are not just for teaching, instructing, or correcting, but it provides us a practice manual. It isn't just a book of "don'ts" but rather it is a book of "dos." That is what is means to train ourselves towards righteousness. Practicing the Word can be done and should be done in our own times with the Lord. This is how we train ourselves to live according to His Word. It is as we learn how to use the Word to disciple ourselves that we are learning how to use it to disciple others.

It is for this purpose that each lesson in this study guide has a section that will demonstrate how to use the Word to disciple your own soul. There will then be a challenge on how to implement that concept daily in your own life, thus teaching and training you how to use the Word to disciple yourself first. The outcome will be an organic flow of using the Word to disciple others.

As with life, the more you put into this, the more you will get out of it! I like to tell my personal clients that when they think they are done with an assignment, to go back and press into it another layer. Be intentional to ask (with expectation) the Holy Spirit to show you more and take it deeper. This practice will often shift you from soul answers to spirit answers.

I pray that this study guide equips you practically by teaching you HOW to disciple, thus empowering you and inspiring you to go and make disciples!

Lisa Schwarz

# LESSON 1

**Read the introduction and chapters 1 & 2**

ENGAGE AND REFLECT:

Take note (or underline in your book) any thing that stuck out to you. Use the space below to respond to the Holy Spirit and what you think He is saying to you personally as you read. This is how we learn to interact with God and the Holy Spirit. Remember, God is not just interested in giving you information, but rather engaging you in a relationship. One of the ways we do this is through conversation with God.

*CHAPTER 1 REFLECTIONS:*

_____
_____
_____
_____
_____
_____
_____
_____

*CHAPTER 2 REFLECTIONS:*

_____
_____
_____
_____
_____
_____
_____
_____

PERSONALIZE:

How would you define discipleship in your words? Did reading these chapters enlighten you in this regard? If so, how?

_____
_____
_____
_____
_____
_____
_____

What has been your discipleship experience? Would you say that it has been effective? How would you have changed it or how would you change it if you could?

_____
_____
_____
_____
_____
_____
_____

EXECUTE:

Think about a current relationship in your life that has the potential to be discipleship… whether it is you being discipled or you doing the discipling. Be intentional to think about how you can put some energy into that relationship. In other words, what action can you take to cultivate connection between you and the other person you are thinking about? Examples could be: a phone call, having coffee, going to lunch, meeting at the park or just going for a walk. Remember, discipleship requires relationship, and relationship requires time. Now... execute! Don't just think about how you should, or would like to... do it! This is the first step to entering into organic discipleship.

## DISCIPLING YOUR OWN SOUL:

I believe the practice of praying through the Scriptures is one of the most powerful tools we have to empower us to walk in victory. Although praying through the Scriptures is often talked about, it is not taught enough. The reality is, His Word provides promises that we can stand on and this knowledge will build confidence in our prayers. It is authoritative, thus affirming us that we are hitting the mark in what we are praying. The Word IS the bullseye! Read the passage below along with the prayer demonstration.

> *"I will extol You, O LORD, for You have lifted me up..."* Psalm 30:1

> *"O yes Lord, I WILL extol You! I WILL exalt You, I WILL speak of You and Your name will ever be upon my lips. I WILL speak of Your goodness all the days of my life and I declare and decree that I will forever be magnifying You in all I do and say. For You are worthy of exalting and there is nothing above You. I declare all things in my life are subject to You... for You ARE Lord of all of me. I agree that You HAVE indeed lifted me up, You have set me high upon a rock, You have exalted me above my enemy, and lifted up my head. I am NOT downcast, I am NOT feeble, I am NOT weak or willowing, but I am lifted up! I am seated with You in the heavenlies and my soul soars with You. Thank you, God, for placing me high upon the Rock of Jesus Christ. I will stand in Your Divine positioning with confidence because of Your hand that lifted me. In Jesus' name, amen."*

What did you notice through this demonstration? Where did my confidence come from? Do I have the right to pray that boldly?

_____
_____
_____
_____

How do you think this prayer might affect my day if I were to pray it morning, noon and night?

How am I forcing my soul to line up with the Spirit? How am I teaching my soul to maintain a posture of praise?

YOUR TURN:

Take some time to pray the prayer demonstration… it's ok if you want to tweak it to make it your own. Just stay confident in your authority to speak boldly into your own soul. If you did this every day for a week, how do you think it might affect you? What effect do you want it to have?

_____

_____

_____

_____

_____

_____

_____

After doing this every day for a week, answer the following.

What affect did praying this every day have on you?

_____

_____

_____

_____

_____

_____

_____

# LESSON 2

**Read Chapters 3 & 4**

ENGAGE AND RELFECT:

Take note (or underline in your book) any thing that stuck out to you. Use the space below to respond to the Holy Spirit and what you think He is saying to you personally as you read. This is how we learn to interact with God and the Holy Spirit. Remember, God is not just interested in giving you information, but rather engaging you in a relationship. One of the ways we do this is through conversation with God.

## CHAPTER 3 REFLECTIONS:

## CHAPTER 4 REFLECTIONS:

*The Study Guide for* Discipleship: From Information to Execution

PERSONALIZE:

Think about the spiritual foundation that has been laid in your own life. What played a part of in the laying of that foundation? Would you say that your foundation has been established more by programs, or by people?

_____
_____
_____
_____
_____
_____
_____

After reading about how Jesus made disciples, do you see ways that discipleship processes around you reflect His example? Do you see ways/processes/or attempts that are different? How are they different, and what are they lacking?

_____
_____
_____
_____
_____
_____
_____

EXECUTE:

Take some time to consider why you do what you do. What kind of spiritual ROI do you see from your spiritual "investments"? In other words, where are you sowing your seed? Make a list of all that you are doing to grow in your walk with God. Pray through that list and ask God to reveal which ones are bringing a return. Remember, we must be intentional in where we sow our seed so be willing to let some things go!

## DISCIPLING YOUR OWN SOUL:

The Scriptures are useful for training yourself toward righteousness. Actions start by training the mind. Consider the passages below in training the mind to think according to the kingdom and keep your mind stayed upon the things of God and seeking His will for your life.

> *"For "who has known the mind of the Lord that he may instruct Him?" But we have the mind of Christ" 1 Corinthians 2:16*
>
> *"If any of you lacks wisdom, let him ask of God, who gives to all liberally and without reproach, and it will be given to him." James 1:5*
>
> *"And do not be conformed to this world, but be transformed by the renewing of your mind, that you may prove what is that good and acceptable and perfect will of God." Romans 12:2*

Read the declarations below to train your own thoughts to think the thoughts of God. Remember, this is about declaring what is true, not necessarily what you think or feel. Note that I have actually just used the Scriptures to be my declarations. I also use them to be points of praise! Again, this is how I can be sure that I am declaring Truth and hitting the bullseye. As you read them, try placing your hand on your own head.

> *"I declare and decree that I have the mind of Christ... that Christ is in me and therefore His mind is in me. I think like Him, and I have knowledge of Him. My thoughts are not my own, but rather they are thoughts of God!"*
>
> *"God, I thank You that You give me wisdom generously without finding any fault. That the moment I seek Your wisdom, You release it. I receive Your wisdom and I walk in it!"*
>
> *"I declare that I am no longer given to this world, but I AM renewing my mind even in this moment and therefore I AM being transformed. I thank You, God, that I am able to easily recognize what is best and I understand Your ways."*

Pick at least one of these Scriptures to use daily as a declaration to your own mind. You can write out the declaration or just let the Holy Spirit guide you each day. Be sure to touch your head as you declare every day!

After doing this every day for a week, answer the following.
What affect did praying this every day have on you?

_____

_____

_____

_____

_____

_____

_____

_____

*The Study Guide for* Discipleship: From Information to Execution

# LESSON 3

**Read Chapters 5 & 6**

ENGAGE AND RELFECT:

Take note (or underline in your book) any thing that stuck out to you. Use the space below to respond to the Holy Spirit and what you think He is saying to you personally as you read. This is how we learn to interact with God and the Holy Spirit. Remember, God is not just interested in giving you information, but rather engaging you in a relationship. One of the ways we do this is through conversation with God.

*CHAPTER 5 REFLECTIONS:*

*CHAPTER 6 REFLECTIONS:*

*The Study Guide for* Discipleship: From Information to Execution

PERSONALIZE:

After reading more in depth the "see one, do one, teach one" concept, write in your own words why you think all three steps are important in teaching someone to master something.

_____
_____
_____
_____
_____
_____
_____
_____

Think about times when you have experienced each of the three "steps" in your personal growth with Christ. Of the three, which one do you think you have experienced the most? Which one do you think has been the most effective? Why?

_____
_____
_____
_____
_____
_____
_____

When considering the idea of being organically discipled by your culture… what cultures have you been discipled by? Think about which ones you were intentional to immerse yourself into and which ones were just parts of the "system" you've be exposed to.

_____
_____

*The Study Guide for* Discipleship: From Information to Execution

_____
_____
_____
_____
_____
_____
_____

What are you currently doing to immerse yourself into a culture where you will be organically discipled in the ways of the kingdom?

_____
_____
_____
_____
_____
_____
_____

EXECUTE:

Create an opportunity where you can disciple someone this week by demonstration. This could be as simple as showing someone how to bake, or change a tire, or make something. Be sure to also invite that person to partner with you, thus giving them the opportunity to actually DO what you have demonstrated.

## DISCIPLING YOUR OWN SOUL:

Let's take a look at how we can learn more about who we are and the character of Christ that is in us. Since we are created in the image of God, we know that God has put it IN us to be like Him. When we shift from just learning about God's ways to learning about His heart, we are actually learning more about who WE are. There are many Scriptures that teach us about the heart and character of God.

> *"But the fruit of the Spirit is love, joy, peace, longsuffering, kindness, goodness, faithfulness, gentleness, self-control. Against such there is no law." Galatians 5:22-23*

This verse reveals to us the nature of Christ and what that nature LOOKS LIKE. I can use this verse to agree with God in who HE is by praying back to Him.

> *"God you are the very essence of love, joy, peace, longsuffering, kindness, goodness, faithfulness, gentleness, and self-control. This is who you are and what You look like."*

I can then take the authority to enforce this same character in my own life. The key here is to stand on the side of victory. In other words, if God is in me, then I can claim these traits over my life, even if I don't see evidence of them. By doing so, I am enforcing what is true to manifest. This is what it means to call those things which do not exist as though they did. (Romans 4:17)

Ok, so let me demonstrate what this would look like...

> *"God, I thank you that I am filled with the fullness of Your Holy Spirit and that with Your Spirit comes Your nature: love, joy, peace, longsuffering, kindness, goodness, faithfulness, gentleness, and self-control. I receive your nature and I loose your nature. May your fruit be seen and evident in my life as I walk in love, joy, peace, longsuffering, kindness, goodness, faithfulness, gentleness, and self-control."*

Take a moment and declare that for yourself.

Now, let's go further and add action to enforce this truth to be seen. Remember, God has already put this nature in us…so we don't have to pray for it, we simply need to receive it, declare it, and then walk in it! We see it, the DO it!

Ok, so take some time to think and pray about which one of these traits of the spirit are the most difficult for you to walk in. Once you have identified the top one or two, start by breathing those traits in as you pray to receive and loose. We are not able to exemplify what we aren't lining up with.

Examples:
> *"God, I receive your patience and longsuffering, I breath it in and exhale shortness and frustration…I rebuke any flesh that would not suffer long and I release Your Spirit the suffers long."*

*"God I thank you that Your joy is IN me...I breath in Your joy and I loose depression and despair...all darkness is fleeing in the presence of Your joy that is in me!"*

After doing this, I would choose an action that would force me to exemplify those traits. So, I might choose to look in the mirror and smile while I claim joy, or spend time dancing for 10 minutes. Or I might choose to engage with someone or something that typically would challenge my patience for the purpose of practicing longsuffering. These actions are an important step for training yourself in righteousness!

Ok, so this is your assignment. Walk through the process I just demonstrated using Galatians 5:22-23 EVERY DAY for the next week.

What affect did this exercise have on you after a week?

_____
_____
_____
_____
_____
_____
_____
_____

Discipling others: Consider how you might use this passage to minister truth to someone else. For example, if someone comes to you struggling with joy or peace, etc., how could this process be used to disciple them? This is the "teach one" step!

# LESSON 4

**Read Chapters 7 & 8**

ENGAGE AND RELFECT:

Take note (or underline in your book) any thing that stuck out to you. Use the space below to respond to the Holy Spirit and what you think He is saying to you personally as you read. This is how we learn to interact with God and the Holy Spirit. Remember, God is not just interested in giving you information, but rather engaging you in a relationship. One of the ways we do this is through conversation with God.

*CHAPTER 7 REFLECTIONS:*

*CHAPTER 8 REFLECTIONS:*

PERSONALIZE:

Take a moment to list all the people you currently seek counsel from on a regular basis. (This can be spiritual counsel or otherwise)

_____
_____
_____
_____
_____
_____
_____
_____

How would your life be different without the counsel of these people?

_____
_____
_____
_____
_____
_____
_____
_____

To the same degree, we should also seek the counsel of the Lord. Would you say that this is easier or harder for you than seeking counsel from people? Why or why not?

_____
_____
_____
_____
_____

*The Study Guide for* Discipleship: From Information to Execution

___

Think about areas in your life where you are a Timothy, and areas where you are a Paul. How is being a Timothy important to being a Paul?

___

Name a person that you are currently a "Paul" to. What would you say is your biggest challenge in being a Paul?

___

EXECUTE:

Spend some time writing thank you notes to those who have poured into you. Be sure to express your gratitude and share some specific ways they have impacted you.

## DISCIPLING YOUR OWN SOUL:

One of my favorite ways to disciple the soul is to engage the body. The Bible is very active and is filled with action verbs. This week is all about acting out whatever any particular verse is saying. Sounds fun, right?! Ok, let me tell you how I learned how powerful this is. When my children were little and I homeschooled them, I taught them verses by adding actions to "act" the verse out. It was how I taught a 2 year old what certain words meant, by showing them through action. It was powerful and I was pleasantly surprised at not only how well I remembered verses, but how I felt what they meant!

Before we go on, let me remind you that the enemy is engaging your flesh every day. In fact, he works THROUGH flesh. This is another reason why choosing to actively engage your body is important. Remember, the Kingdom of heaven is being taken with force, and with force we MUST take it back! (Matthew 11:12)

Examples:

*"Thus I will bless You while I live; I will lift up my hands in Your name."* Psalm 63:4

In this case, I would personally take time to pause and bless God in my own words, and then I would actually raise my arms up as I said His name. Ok, think with me for a minute, if we simply paused every 30 minutes throughout the day to say the name of Jesus and raise our hands, what kind of impact do you think it would have?! Just a thought!

How about this one...

*"He makes my feet like the feet of deer, And set me on my high places."* Psalm 18:33.

When I am feeling insecure or stifled, I love to act this verse out. I might touch my feet, or run in place... and then I will stand on a chair or a table to claim the rest! I promise you, the enemy will flee when you speak the Word out loud, AND demonstrate it regularly.

Now it is your turn. Take some time and pick 5 verses out of the Psalms that have action verbs. Act those verses out every day for a week.

What affect did this exercise have on you after a week?

_____
_____
_____
_____
_____
_____
_____
_____

Discipling others: When I minister to others, I tend to ask them to do things physically. In doing so, I am enforcing faith to rise up. It is amazing how having someone stand on a chair can set them free from fear or from feeling insignificant. Or having them raise their hands can empower them in a moment. Ask the Lord to reveal an opportunity to minister to someone this week by engaging them in to the actions of the Word. Be ready!

*The Study Guide for* Discipleship: From Information to Execution

# LESSON 5

**Read Chapters 9 & 10**

ENGAGE AND RELFECT:

Take note (or underline in your book) any thing that stuck out to you. Use the space below to respond to the Holy Spirit and what you think He is saying to you personally as you read. This is how we learn to interact with God and the Holy Spirit. Remember, God is not just interested in giving you information, but rather engaging you in a relationship. One of the ways we do this is through conversation with God.

*CHAPTER 9 REFLECTIONS:*

*CHAPTER 10 REFLECTIONS:*

PERSONALIZE:

Which generation would you say you related to the most? Why?

___

Were you challenged to consider ways you could connect with the opposite generation more effectively? What can you do this week to connect?

___

Why is important to disciple yourself to look like who God made you to be? How does this free you up from what you have possibly been told or how you have been guided or molded?

___

*The Study Guide for* Discipleship: From Information to Execution

What is the key to discipling someone according to where God is taking them? Why is this so important? Do you think this makes it easier or harder to disciple? Why or why not?

EXECUTE:

Do something intentional this week to connect with someone of a different generation. Seek to learn from them and them take some time to journal about your experience.

## DISCIPLING YOUR OWN SOUL:

For our last week, let's take a look at how we can personalize the Scriptures. To do this, you simply speak through a given verse in first person. So instead of reading it as if it is being spoken to a random person, you are receiving it as if it were only written to you… and for you. This is a great way to shift your thinking into the truth of your Christ identity.

For Example:

> *"For God has not given us a spirit of fear, but of power and of love and of a sound mind."* 2 Timothy 1:7

Read how I take this verse and apply it to myself by speaking it in first person.

> *"God, you have not given my a spirit of fear, but I have a spirit of power and of love and of a sound mind…"*

I might take it further to declare it…

> *"I declare and decree that I walk in the power of God, His love and that my thoughts are clear as a bell… there is no fear in me and declare any fear a liar… you are not of God!"*

Now, I can also insert my name and look into a mirror to speak into myself (third person)

> *"Lisa, You have the mind of Christ. You are filled with power and love and are sound minded. There is no fear in you, and you walk in confidence because you know that God is with you."*

Remember the power of adding motions… so try touching your head or nodding at yourself as you are saying this in the mirror. You could make a muscle to represent power, or rub your heart when declaring His love in you. It sounds corny, I know… but trust me it works! The enemy gets us to engage physically, so why shouldn't we do it with God?

To expound on this, try reading the verse in alternative versions to help you understand the depths of what God is saying.

> *"For God did not give us a spirit of timidity or cowardice or fear, but [He has given us a spirit] of power and of love and of sound judgment and personal discipline [abilities that result in a calm, well-balanced mind and self-control]. 1 Timothy 2:7 Amplified*

Here's how I might receive this…

> *"There is no cowardice or fearfulness in me, but God, You have filled me with strength and power. I am not confused or cloudy, but I practice sound judgment and am disciplined. I am not given to my emotions or my circumstances, but instead I am calm and even tempered!"*

See how that expanded my declaration?

Ok, here is one more...

> *"For we are His workmanship, created in Christ Jesus for good works, which God prepared beforehand that we should walk in them." Ephesians 2:10*
>
> *"I AM the handiwork of God created through Christ and I produce good works! Everything about me was prepared and in place before I was born and I walk in the fullness of who I am in Christ and fruit comes forth from my life."*

In the mirror (third person)

> *"Lisa, you are the workmanship of God... you are being was crafted by His fingers with the purpose of producing good works. There is nothing that you will encounter that He has not prepared you for ahead of time. You walk in His plan and you live out His purpose."*

Ok, so this is your assignment for this week. You can use these verses, or pick your own. Be sure to practice first person and third person, and use a mirror. And don't forget to add motions when you canJ

What affect did this exercise have on you after a week?

_____
_____
_____
_____
_____
_____
_____
_____

Discipling Others: Think about how you can use this concept when ministering to others. You can use their name as you are praying for them...

> *"Jane, you have not a spirit of timidity..."*

Try also having them repeat only saying, "*I have not a spirit of timidity*," thus forcing their minds to come into alignment with what is true.

# CONCLUSION

My heart's desire is that this study guide not only personalized the concept of discipleship for you, but that it also taught you HOW to use the Scriptures to train yourself into the character of Christ. I want you to be set free from the flesh and live out the liberty and beauty of the spirit. It is so frustrating to simply have information, but not know how to turn it into action. Knowledge without application is just facts, but with application it is wisdom.

I pray that this study guide provided practical examples and that you received more than just information, but that you saw demonstration even through writing. As you learn to use the Scriptures to disciple your own soul, you will be surprised how you will organically begin to disciple others. It will not be forced, but will be a joy!

Now, go and do it! Go make disciples among the nations!

PLEASE VISIT MY WEBSITE…
- To download the audio, "Using the Scriptures to Minister" to learn more about how to use the Word to disciple.
- If you are interested in learning more about discipleship, or would like to host a 6 week study, workshop, or conference on this topic.
- If you would like to write a testimony about this book and study guide.
- If you are interested in personal counseling or life coaching.
- To learn more about other books and teachings.

www.lisa-schwarz.com

Follow me on Facebook at Lisa Schwarz or Twitter @iamlisaschwarz or @C8Ministries

Made in the USA
Columbia, SC
13 January 2022